Not all senior executives get the job they think they deserve...

...often it is not the most experienced or most talented executive that gets the job...

...it's the most prepared!

Contents

A note from the author

One of the most distressing things about working in the recruitment and executive search markets is seeing the perfect candidate apply for a position that they agree is their perfect job, only to then see them fall at the first or second interview hurdle, simply because they weren't prepared for what was about to come.

We knew they were a superb fit, they knew they were a superb fit, but they threw it all away by not spending enough time and effort proving to the interviewer that they were a superb fit.

Of course we can add value to a certain extent, by providing specific insight into the position, the person, the opportunity and the 'hot buttons' that the interviewer is looking to be hit. However, in the interview, the responsibility to perform to your best ability is ultimately yours.

The drop in activity in C-suite career moves over the last 5 years means that many executives are more than a little ring rusty in the dark arts of the job interview.

No doubt you've led recruitment drives within the organisations you've previously been involved with but, if you are honest with yourself, really honest, when it comes to representing yourself in an interview situation, how prepared are you really?

Now I am aware that the subject of interview technique has earned large numbers of people even larger sums of money through the publishing of the plethora of 'How to' books… but to be honest, our experience is that most of these are more about the publishing money than providing any real, useful advice.

What follows is our observations that are genuinely evidenced based. They come from real, up-to-date experience of working with senior executives in their job searches and our clients in their own search for talented executives. So, as well as being based on our expertise, they are also based on what really works in the real world.

As the UK economic climate continues to improve and GDP figures show more robust growth, confidence is quickly returning to all levels of the labour market and the search for executive talent is no exception to this upward trend.

Getting an interview is one of the key targets in a job search campaign. You should never forget that to be invited to interview is an important measure of success in itself. But a great deal still depends on how skilfully you handle yourself at the interview and whether you succeed in getting your key messages across.

Nigel Brewster,
Partner,
Brewster Pratap Recruitment Group

08

So, you took the call from the headhunter. You sent a copy of your CV. You went to meet them to talk meaningfully through your experience, capabilities and future plans. You drank their coffee (and laughed at their jokes) and a week or so later you received the call to arrange an interview with their client.

Well done so far, but now what are you going to do?

Not totally sure? Well, that's what this book is about.

010

Personal Branding

Personal branding

Personal branding... really? Yes, perhaps even before thinking about your CV and before meeting the headhunter (if indeed, one is involved) you really ought to have thought about your own brand. You are probably already experienced in managing corporate or organisational brands. Perhaps you are directly responsible for one, or have developed and grown one, or you might even calculate the value of one on the balance sheet, but have you ever thought about your own personal brand?

Personal branding… So, what's it all about then?

It's your reputation. It's about transmitting who you are, what you do and how you do it. It's about making your mark by being yourself — and by this we mean your ***'best'*** self (or as I prefer to describe it...the person your parents like to think you are).

Think of your personal brand as your calling card — your unique promise of value (and in the case of CVs and job interviews, your promise of value to a department, a team and an organisation). It's what you're known for and how people experience you (but not spin or untruths) you need to stick to it, keep reinforcing it and ultimately live it.

Let's start at the beginning… a personal brand is in many ways synonymous with your reputation. It refers to the way other people see you. Are you a genius? An expert? Are you trustworthy? What do you represent? What do you stand for? What ideas and notions pop up as soon as someone hears your name?

A personal brand can enhance your recognition as an expert in your field, establish your reputation and credibility, build your self-confidence and, of course, advance your career.

Well-executed personal brands create a strong, consistent, and specific association between you and the perceived value you offer. If this is all new to you, personal branding typically begins with establishing an inventory of your core competencies, expertise, abilities, beliefs and core values.

Personal branding consists of three elements

1. **Value proposition:**
What principles or beliefs do you stand for?

2. **Differentiation:**
What skills or talents make you stand out?

3. **Marketability:**
What makes you compelling?
(Or, why would you be a good colleague?)

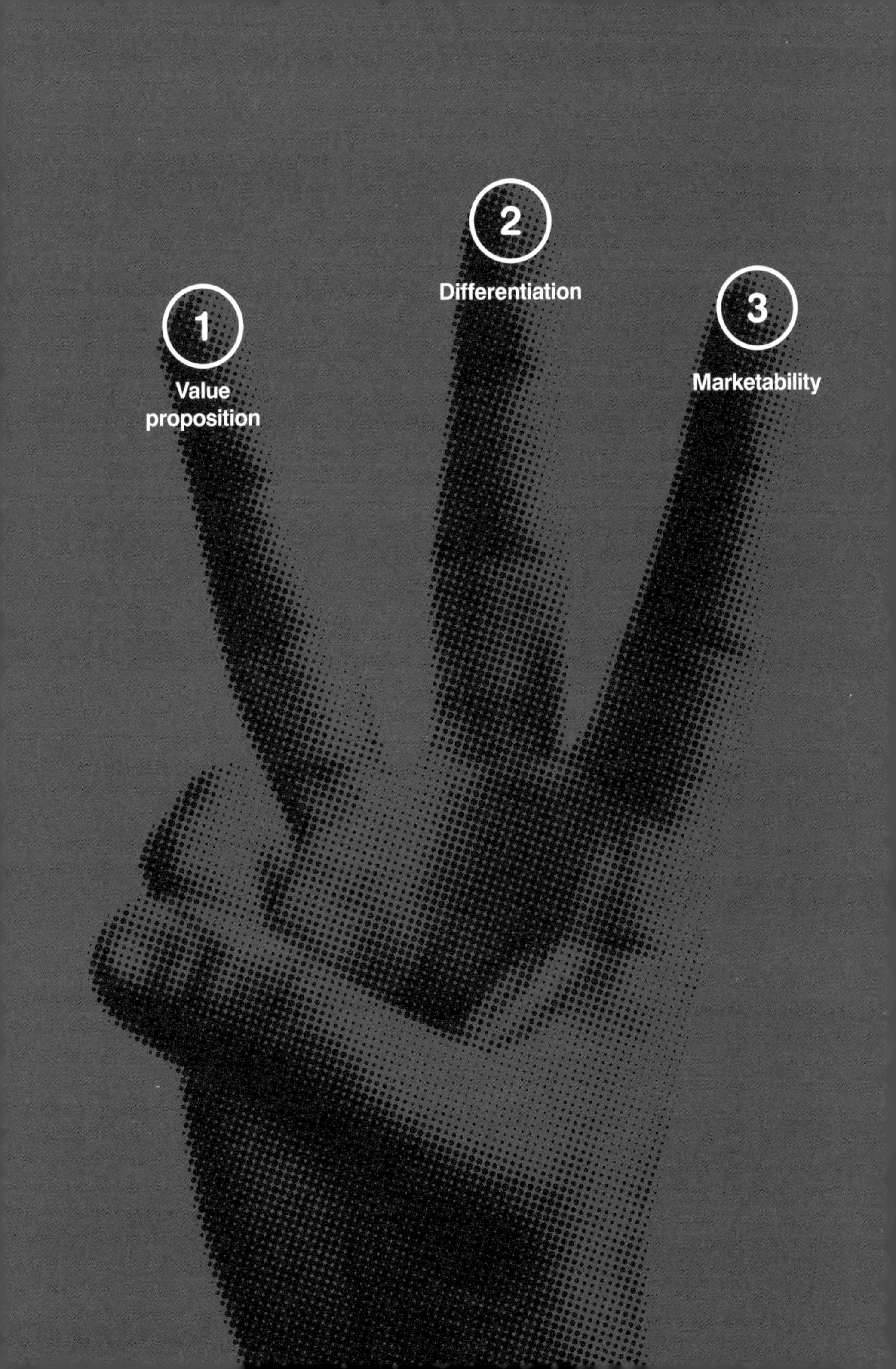
1
Value proposition
2
Differentiation
3
Marketability

Probably, the most important point to note about your personal brand is that you already have one.

It is very likely that the people you work with know you, not by the person you are but, instead by your brand. Are you honest, scary, professional, funny? You already have a personal brand but it is very unlikely any interviewer will know about it before you arrive, other than through your CV or your actions so far. They will learn about it from what you say and the way you say it at interview.

Like all brands, the most powerful are created through resonance and repetition, so make sure your CV message is consistent with your interview brand and think seriously about what you want your brand to be.

Also, if you haven't yet updated your CV, make sure when you do, it reflects your personal brand. If you are going to use a 'Personal Statement' on your CV (you know… that opening paragraph that is on most CV templates) then use the words and statements that immediately demonstrate your value proposition, your areas of differentiation and your marketability.

If this all sounds a bit too 'American' for you, just think of it like this...having a clear sense of self that encompasses your beliefs, values, skills, experience and general style is pretty much essential to successfully communicating who you are. If it makes it easier, forget the term 'Personal Brand' and think of it as 'Who am I?'

Spend some time thinking about your personal brand, our key pointers are:

Decide and lay out your core values

How would you like potential employers to think of you? Because your personal brand is built from the thoughts, words and reactions of other people, it's shaped by how you present yourself. This is something that you have control over. Values are the easiest things to present and have people identify with, so start there. Are you the sort of person who puts ethics above everything else?

Become good at what you do

Every good brand involves the notion of expertise. You need to create the perception that you are very good at what you do.

Market your personality

You need to think hard about how you act. You should have a clearly identifiable personality so that people can easily feel like they know you personally, even if they've never met you. Your style of delivery should be as unique as any other aspect of your personal brand. This doesn't mean you need to sit down and consciously think how to be different, it will happen naturally.

Are you kind and unusually enthusiastic? Are you witty and raw? Are you confident and crusading? Remember, the knack is to be someone that is appointable!

A strong, clear, understandable and repeatable personal brand will help an interviewer get a better understanding of why they should appoint you. You already have one, but make sure it's one that you're proud of.

Preparing for interviews

1

Back to basics

2

Research

3

Preparing an agenda

1 Firstly, back to basics

Don't ever forget – an interview is a two-way exchange of information

Obviously the interviewer is trying to find out about you, but you're also sizing them up, forming an impression of what it will be like to work with and for them, and collecting information to aid your decision as to whether you would like to join them. Given this two-way exchange you must be clear about what the interviewer learns about you.

The interviewer's agenda is usually to:

- Get a clearer picture of your experiences and capabilities
- Hear examples of how you worked in the past, what you really did and how you really did it
- Get an accurate idea of how you match their needs (both in the short and longer term)
- Compare you with other good applicants.

So, with this in mind, your aim should always be to:

- Present compelling evidence of your experience, skills, knowledge and your ability to deliver (both in the short and longer term)
- Reveal your personality and style (your personal brand) and your ability to work well with others
- Assess how the organisation meets your needs on job content, working environment, culture, style and career prospects
- Get the interviewers / organisation excited about employing you.

An interviewer will be looking at your competence (have you got the knowledge and experience and skills to do the job?) and your compatibility (does your working style fit the organisation and particularly the people you will be working with?).

Typically, other than an initial 'first impressions' assessment, at the first interview, the main focus will be evaluating your competence. This is usually pretty evident as their main agenda, although they may start to form an opinion on compatibility as well. In follow-up interviews your compatibility is likely to be a much more important aspect of the discussion.

As a Senior Manager, Executive or Business Leader, you may well be more familiar with the interview process from the other side of the desk (as an interviewer) and now you can make this experience work for you by using your knowledge of what interviewers are looking for, and why.

An exercise which is often useful is to reflect on some situations where you have interviewed people yourself. Think about what you were looking for when searching for the right person. Spend some time thinking about what in particular impressed you about people that were successful in interviews and why the candidates who failed at interview didn't do themselves justice or how they let themselves down.

This exercise will remind you of some valuable themes and help you position the interviewer not as an awkward interrogator, but as someone whose prime concern is to evidence how individuals match criteria agreed in advance, and to find the right person to join the team.

The best interviews are performed by those who have done their homework on the vacancy, on the business and, as much as possible, the culture (more on this later). It is important to give a good impression that is consistent with the one that has been created on paper.

2 Research

It should go without saying, but you need to be well prepared and fully briefed on the organisation you are visiting.

As a minimum, always conduct these interview 'pre-flight checks'	
Make sure you are familiar with the job description and understand the person specification. Draw up a list of questions, observations and points for discussion.	✓
Make sure you confirm your attendance (either directly or with the recruitment company).	✓
Check the location (obvious, but don't make the mistake of going to the wrong site of large corporates or use sat nav and realise that the postcode address takes you to the local sorting office). Yes, it happens frequently. Also make sure you're aware of car parking arrangements.	✓
Make sure you know the anticipated length and type of job interview, what sort of interview it is (e.g. panel interview) and whether there will be any tests.	✓
If a headhunter is involved, get all the background information you can before your interview with the client company (why is the role available and why have they been instructed etc).	✓
Make sure you know the names and job titles of the interviewers and, if possible, look them up on 'LinkedIn' to see what you can find out about them (don't worry about them knowing you've looked them up - it proves you've done your homework).	✓
Make sure you have done some relevant background research, for example; statutory accounts, most recent share price, a thorough run through the business website, a 'Google' search of news articles about the business, a similar search on the business' industry sector.	✓

Obvious I know, but preparation and research is absolutely essential. Given how potentially life changing a new executive role can be, we still find the number of people who expect to just 'wing it' on the day quite staggering! Research will also help you draw up a list of potential questions for the interviewer that are way beyond the interview crimes of "how many holidays will I get?"

Interview crimes

Gaining an understanding of the challenges the company has faced in the past will help you better understand how your personal experience dealing with similar issues can benefit their business. The more successful you are at presenting yourself as a solution to the company's problems, the more likely you are to get hired.

025

Research will undoubtedly enable you to deal with the question; "So, what do you know about our company?" As a Senior Manager or Executive, you are expected to research a company before applying. Repeating website information won't be good enough, so start by learning the company's values and mission and be prepared to discuss which of your own values are similar. Highlighting a fit between their culture and values and your own personal brand will give you an advantage.

Discuss the company's history. Don't worry about remembering what year it was founded, but knowing whether it's a newly formed organisation or has been around for 50 years is obviously important.

Knowing the CEO's name and those of the key personnel does more than help during the interview, it shows the interviewer that you have a healthy interest in the company's leadership and in wanting to know what their responsibilities are. It lets the interviewer know that you are genuinely interested in the work that lies ahead and that your interest in joining the Executive Team goes beyond personal ambition.

026

Before you go anywhere near the interview you need to be able to identify the key points that you want the interviewer to learn about you (see Preparing an Agenda on page 28) and how you're going to get them across using some sort of narrative or story.

Stories are good...really? Yes, in interviews, as in most of life, tall stories are bad, but stories are definitely good. Human beings are subconsciously familiar with the convention of 'stories', in that they have a beginning, a middle and an end.

From the dawn of modern mankind, people have sat around campfires and told stories. There is something comforting and familiar with the convention of beginning, middle and end. How often have you heard someone say "I didn't like that film (or book) because it had a funny ending?" That will usually be because it didn't follow the beginning, middle and end convention. But why is this in any way relevant to the job interview?

Well, the interviewer will get a far better, more rounded view of your performance and your answers if they follow a beginning, middle and end convention, BUT, make sure that your answers are never more than about one minute long – at the absolute most. Stories are good, but short stories are best. The real skill here is to give the interviewer the subconscious comfort and familiarity of a classic story convention, in an answer that is less than a minute long.

027

HOT TIP

Stories are powerful and are what people remember most (as long as they are not tall stories!)

3 Preparing an agenda

029

In your day-to-day work you would usually prepare an agenda for an important internal or external meeting right? And particularly if you knew you only had a certain amount of time to cover quite a few points. Depending on your style this might be a formal agenda, or it might be a few prompts on a piece of paper. Whatever your preference, I'm sure you'd normally have some form of preparation?

Preparing for an executive job interview is no different. You may well have over 20 years' of relevant experience that you could talk through and you will probably have (if you've done some decent background research) about 30 minutes worth of questions and discussion about the business, the sector or the market. With all of this bubbling around in your brain, coupled with a little bit of nervousness, it's often almost impossible to get some sort of clear order to your part of the interview.

So, firstly think about the experiences and achievements you want to cover. Which aspects of your experience and achievements must you get across? Not all will be relevant, so which ones are best matched to what you think the organisation is looking for and which will you use as evidence?

Once you've thought of examples that demonstrate these experiences and achievements, add your list of questions about the job description and person specification. Add to this the questions that have been flagged up by your research.

Put them in a logical or meaningful order and to make sure you cover (and remember) them, write clearly and concisely...

...As if by magic...there you have it - your agenda for the interview!

030

It's not enough just to say you have a particular skill or knowledge, provide evidence to back up your claim (more on this later on page 58). When you have identified a list of examples to illustrate each of your skills and you have thought about what you will say when you talk about them, make sure that they form part of your agenda. We have lost count of the number of times an interviewer has not managed to get a full picture of someone's experience because they ran out of time, or spent too long discussing one part of their experience. Preparing an agenda will help you tick off the points you want to cover… and before you ask "Are you really suggesting I take an agenda into a job interview!?"… the answer is 'Yes'. But, obviously don't write 'Agenda' on the top of it!

HOT TIP

Prepare a list of the things that you want to cover, both parts of your experience but also things that you want to know more about. Keep it in some sort of file or folio that looks professional.

On commencing the interview ask permission to use it by saying something like "as part of my research before today, I've prepared some notes and a couple of questions, is it OK if I refer to them during this interview?"
As you are attending a job interview, not a memory test, the answer will always be "Yes, of course" and now in one fell swoop you have:

A **proved to the interviewer that you have done some preparation**

B **proved that you are organised and professional**

C **given yourself a fool proof set of prompts to use should your mind go blank due to nervousness.**

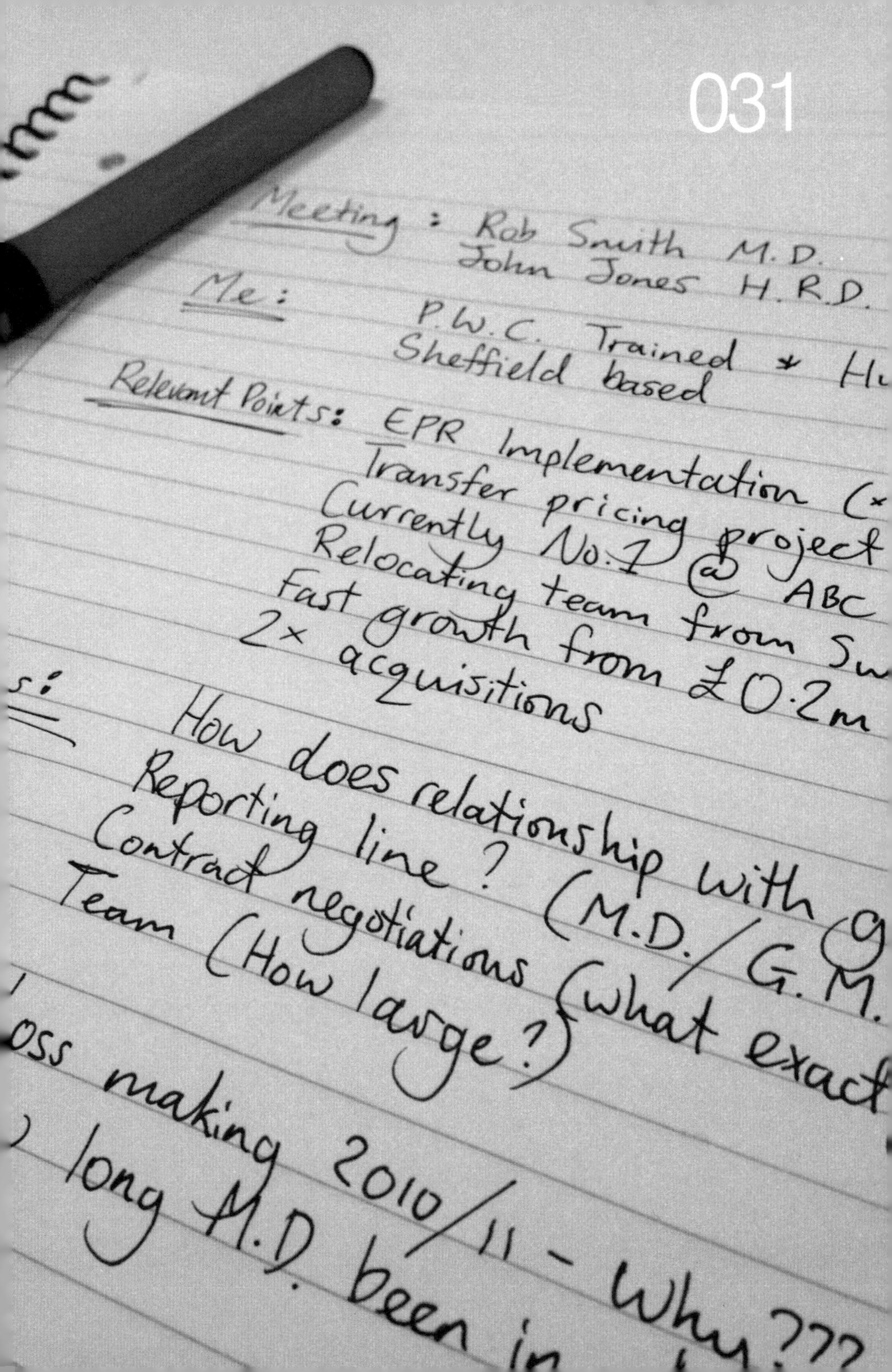
Meeting: Rob Smith M.D.
John Jones H.R.D.
Me:
P.W.C. Trained * H
Sheffield based
Relevant Points: EPR Implementation
Transfer pricing project
Currently No.1 @ ABC
Relocating team from Sw
Fast growth from £0.2m
2× acquisitions
How does relationship with
Reporting line? (M.D./G.M.
Contract negotiations (what exact
Team (How large?)
oss making 2010/11 - Why???
long M.D. been in

031

NERVES

033

A QUICK WORD ABOUT Nerves

As your career develops and you take more senior roles, nervousness before an interview can sometimes feel like some sort of weakness that your 'junior self' used to suffer from but nowadays you should be better than that. Remember: pre-interview nerves are good.

Nervousness is a basic physiological response to the prospect of not being in full control of a forthcoming situation. Nervousness proves that you are bothered about how you come across, how you portray your skills and experience and fundamentally proves that you are interested in the job. If you aren't even just a little bit nervous, have a serious think about whether you are really interested in going through the process at all. From my experience:

Lack of Nerves = Lack of Interest

A certain amount of nervousness before a job interview is normal so be prepared to deal with it. Any interviewer will usually make allowances for nervousness and the unnatural nature of the situation.

By preparing an agenda with the key points you want to cover, you will feel more confident and won't be caught out if your mind does go blank for a moment.

034

Questions you may be asked

035

036

Here are some themes and topics you are very likely to be asked in an interview. We have grouped them into four areas with six questions in each for ease. This is not intended to be exhaustive but should give you a good starting point. Prepare the point you want to make and be sure that it reflects the personal brand that you are trying to consistently convey in your answers (but obviously don't learn them word for word!)

Your job attitudes

What do you look for in a job?

Why you want to work for this organisation?

What do you want to avoid in your next job?

What are your career objectives beyond this next role?

What is important to you?

What motivates you?

Your last position

What did you like most / least about your last job?

Name a couple of problems you resolved that had previously been overlooked

Tell me about two things you learnt in your last position

How would you describe your relationship with your current / former boss?

How have you developed in your last role?

What's your current personal development plan?

About you

Tell me about yourself (see later on for some specific thoughts on this one!)

If you could start your career over again, what would you do differently?

Why are you looking to move jobs?

How would your colleagues describe you?

Which part of your colleagues' description would you disagree with?

What is your style of management?

About your accomplishments

What are your biggest three accomplishments in your career to date?

What size of budget are you used to handling?

What can you bring to this position?

Give an example where you managed change in difficult circumstances.

What has been difficult about your previous roles?

What are you most proud of?

Gaps in your CV

hello, anybody there?

You will need to explain gaps in employment. If you worked in a temporary capacity but didn't put it on your CV, know the details of which companies you worked with, what you did for them and the length of the assignments. If you did not work, but did search for a job, give some examples of the research you did regarding job opportunities and the process you went through to find the position.

Reasons for leaving

Prepare to discuss the reasons you left your previous jobs. If it was for a better opportunity, explain why it was better. If you left involuntarily, present the reason in the most positive light you can. Make sure your responses are honest and be positive. Be prepared because chances are, you will be asked.

039

A Quick Word About Big to Little

'Big to Little' is a handy technique that you can use to illustrate the depth of experience an interviewer will be looking for in an executive interview (and will demonstrate both strategic and operational experience).
'Big' refers to a high level overview of subjects, themes, strategies and areas and allows you to paint a broad brush picture of your understanding and experience. 'Little' refers to one or two detailed descriptions of what you actually did as an example of a subject area. Start 'Big' with an overview of your experience – just a short description of overall scope and depth. Then, follow up with smaller details and examples. Probably two to four specific achievements, projects or highlights.

'Big to Little' can be really useful (when used together) simply because if your answer is only about 'Big' descriptions you may appear to be too far away from the detail and not be capable of doing what you say. If your answer is only about 'Little' descriptions you may appear too operational for the executive role in question.

Five key interview tips

Think about the following to fine-tune your preparation

THE O.E.M.'S S.L.A.S
MEANT WE HAD TO REDESIGN OUR OWN K.P.I.S
WHICH WAS A SLOG FOR THE S.M.T.
AS AT THE TIME
WE WERE IN THE MIDDLE OF A FULL O.R.G. REVIEW

LISTEN to the question

Listen to questions carefully and respond as naturally as you can. Sounds really simple, doesn't it, however it's often the number one reason why people don't progress through an interview process.

In particular, take care not to answer the question that you wished the interviewer had asked you and never answer a question by spewing out a monologue of everything you want the interviewer to learn about you. Just listen carefully and answer the question. The preparation you have made will pay off here as you'll make a better impression if you can present relevant information without being prompted and without too much thinking time. But don't just rely on the interviewers' questions to guide you.

ACCEPT that most interviewers are not very good at interviewing

Professional interviewers may lead you skilfully through the course of an interview but, more often than not, you will be interviewed by Managers or Directors who don't do this for a living. As a result, they may not be very skilled at drawing information out of you.

So, your starting point should be that the person you are meeting is more nervous and less prepared than you are. Be prepared to volunteer key points about yourself if they are not covered by the interviewer's questions and make sure you cover as many of the points on your agenda as possible. Don't let an ill-prepared interviewer hamper you getting your key points across.

043

AVOID clichés, business jargon and acronyms

INTERVIEW TIP 3

- Avoid textbook answers such as "I believe in adding value." A statement like this means nothing whatsoever! Try instead to give examples of how you did!
- Steer clear of clichés and business jargon even if they are in current use such as 'low hanging fruit' or 'no brainer' unless your personal brand is to be Gordon Gekko!
- Try not to use acronyms and abbreviations (unless your interviewer refers to them first) "The OEM's SLAs meant we had to redesign our own KPIs which was a slog for the SMT as at the time we were in the middle of a full ORG review." This is not cool!

HOT TIP

Avoid inconsistency between what you say and the impression you give people. For example, there's no point in saying you value people if you don't mention the impact on people in anything you discuss.

ASK questions (and have some prepared before the interview)

"Have you got any questions?" When you hear this question don't be fooled into thinking that the hard part is over. This is a key part of the interview in which, if you are really smart, you can easily stand out from the crowd. Asking intelligent, relevant questions is really just another part of your assessment. Use it as an opportunity to show that you are interested in a job, that you have done your research and that you have a real grasp on what the job entails and how you've thought about your career.

You should know this already, but just in case... DO NOT ask about pay and benefits. You should try to avoid mentioning them until you reach the final interview stage. If the interviewer brings up the subject, try not to pin yourself down to a definitive figure. Don't be evasive but say something like "Pay and benefits are obviously important to me but I am primarily interested in the opportunity this role represents."

Some questions you can ask:

- What would you like the person you appoint to achieve in the first year?
- What does success look like for this position?
- What is the biggest challenge facing the successful person?
- What is the biggest challenge facing the business?
- Have the objectives of the business changed recently and, if so, why?
- Have there been any major organisational changes recently?
- What would you say are the most exciting things about this business / opportunity?
- How do you see your market evolving over the next 3 years?

045

DON'T turn up empty handed

There are some things that are useful to have with you in the interview however, keep them stored away in something professional that you can take into the meeting with you until they are needed. A conference folder is a way of storing any papers that you want to take to the interview and is always better than rummaging in a packed briefcase or handbag.

We believe you should always take:

- Any information about the job you may have
- The names and titles of the interviewers
- The company phone number (in case you get lost or get stuck in traffic)
- Any important company information or product literature
- A copy of your CV
- Your diary (you may be asked about your availability for the next stage at the end of the interview
- Pen and paper
- Your 'agenda' and any notes of any key points you want to make
- Any relevant references.

046

At the interview

047

Rightly or wrongly people do hire people they like, so try to establish a rapport at the start and greet the interviewer with a smile and a firm handshake (I said firm, NOT some sort of arm wrestle).

You want to be perceived as friendly and make the interviewer feel they would be comfortable if you worked with them. Generally speaking, you should come across as quietly confident and no matter how bad the interviewer is, do not take total charge or interrupt. At the start, try and establish how the interview will proceed and check how much time is available. This will help shape how you will go about covering your agenda.

Be prepared that you may have to drop some of your points if time is limited. Your answers to questions should be relevant, concise and to the point without getting bogged down in detail as this will make your answer wander off the original point. Break up longer explanation stages and speak no more than about one or two minutes at a time, as an absolute maximum.

Your focus should be on how you can contribute to the organisation's success (using examples from your current and previous experience as tools). It's not always a question of 'did you do something well', but also why the task or activity was important to the organisation?
In your preparation, always follow up any point you want to make with the questions 'so what?'

£1.2m increase in sales sounds good, unless of course your target was £10.2m! Context (or the 'so what' factor) is invaluable.

It will help focus the mind, not just on what you did and how you did it, but on the impact it had on the business (top line, bottom, line etc.).

If there are periods of silence, don't feel like you have to fill them. Don't forget, most interviewers don't do it for a living and so, on the thankfully rare occasions that they try be to 'unconventional' by provoking you or trying to make you feel uncomfortable, stay calm and composed. It may be their intention to see how you react as part of their 'interviewer' technique. Thankfully this is rare, but these people do exist.

Listen actively and look interested in what the interviewer is saying or asking you. Observe their reactions to what you are saying. Be positive and enthusiastic without becoming gushing and never criticise your past employer or sound embittered. When you are asked about your current or last organisation, give a balanced picture of both the good and the not so good. If you have had, or are having a particularly bad experience, spend some time to carefully think through your answer to this one in your initial preparation. These are potential 'flash points' that may spill out in the stress situations caused by an interview.

Being aware of body language

Yes, I know that when you were a Junior Manager coming up through the ranks you went on a course about body language, or read a book on it, so you know quite a bit about it already... but, trust me, the executive interview is the place where all your personal body language 'ticks' and unconscious signals will come out.

Firstly, there are many opinions and interpretations of the signals we give unconsciously, so it is important that you consider this aspect of communication. All of us do it all of the time, particularly in situations of stress or uncertain environments of which we are unfamiliar.

What follows is a generally accepted view on the subject but a word of caution is needed.

HOT TIP

Take care not to over-analyse and interpret non-verbal signals. Scratching your chin can sometimes just mean that you have an itch on your chin.

Secondly, and probably more importantly, to those of you whose careers have taken you internationally or globally, body language is culturally dependent. For example, we may interpret someone avoiding eye contact to be less than honest but, in a number of countries and cultures, it is expected behaviour when talking to someone you respect or of higher social status. Our bodies send out a continuous stream of signals and even silence can be loaded with unspoken meanings. We listen with our eyes as much as with our ears.

So, in your interview preparation, think about all of your communication.

A refresh on the 'body language' basics

Words

There have been numerous studies about how important words are in communication. Some suggest that the words people spoke contributed to less than **10% of the impact** or effectiveness in trying to force people's attitudes. Whether you agree with this, or not, it's important to remember this as a concept.

Voice

Loudness, softness, tone, tempo and inflection are generally accepted to account for somewhere between **35 and 40% of our impact**.

Body

Movement, posture, eye contact and facial expression, combined with overall appearance is suggested to contribute up to **55% of the impact** of our communication. To listen effectively you need to learn how to spot any underlying conflict, boredom or discomfort and should be aware of what we are saying with our posture and reduce any negative effects to a whisper rather than a shout.

Eyes

Our eyes are probably the best signal of how we are getting on with someone. Usually we look at people's eyes and faces to show we are listening or to get feedback on what we are saying.

If someone maintains eye contact whilst we are speaking it is at least a signal that they are interested, even if they don't agree with what we are saying. In general conversation listeners look more at the speaker then vice versa.

Subconsciously, listeners are searching for cues that support or contradict the speaker's words. Are they lying? Are they serious? Should I laugh?

People also look at each other more in co-operative relationships and less if the relationship is tense or cold. People who are lying eventually avert their eyes and look down. Admittedly, some people can maintain their gaze when telling a lie but they usually overdo it and reveal a dishonesty with a long, fixed, unnatural stare.

Facial expression and body movements

Most facial expressions last for about half a second to a second. Some can't be caught by the most alert observer but most of us react to facial expressions intuitively, even if we can't explain what causes us to react that way.

When people like each other or are in agreement, their bodies tend to move at the same time or speed or in the same way. They tend to lean forward or backward at the same time, they use similar motions with the arms legs and hands. People seated next to each other who are in agreement tend to cross and uncross their legs at about the same time and assume a similar sitting position.

When people don't agree, their body motion is reversed and the listener might slightly turn away from the speaker. Listeners in a positive mood tend to do things like scratching their chin, run fingers through their hair and look up at the ceiling. Feet and legs often reveal anxiety or even rage with tense posture and nervous leg jiggling.

Assuming a posture similar to someone standing or sitting nearby can reveal the desire to identify with them. In negotiations people sit closer to the table if they are pleased with progress, or further from the table if the talks are either displeasing or frightening.

The most important point about all of this is that your spoken and unspoken messages need to say the same thing. If you claim to be energetic it's no good slumping motionless in the chair. If you claim to be enthusiastic your voice must also be enthusiastic.

A QUICK WORD ABOUT ★ ★ ★ telephone & skype

Much of our advice equally applies to telephone interviews. They key thing to remember is that, no matter how informal they say the conversation is, they'll be assessing you, so don't be seduced and say things you shouldn't. Seize every chance you can to drive home your interest in the job and your relevant skills and experiences (it is even easier to use your pre prepared agenda as the interviewer can't see that you have one in front of you!). The other advice about how you present yourself still applies but with only your voice to sell you it is all the more important to be enthusiastic, relevant and all the other things you strive for in face-to-face meetings.

All of our advice is equally transferable to 'Skype' interviews, so you don't really need to do anything different, however, remember our three golden rules:

1. Do not be tempted to slouch – even in telephone interviews (the interviewer will be able to tell from your tone of voice).

2. On Skype, never, ever forget that you are being watched.

3. Remain professional and be fully prepared well before the call has started. Remain professional and in the 'interview zone' until you are absolutely sure that the interview has finished and the interviewer has logged off the call.

Types of interview

Latin: *Interviewus stressfullus (The classic panel interview)*

057

Panel interviews

Panel interviews are increasingly common and simply mean that several people will interview you at one time. This panel, or team approach, means that many different people interview you and then get together to debate whether they like you well enough to hire you.

Most people find them a bit of an ordeal but this is typically because many panel interviews use competency interview frameworks and not because of the panel itself. (See page 58 for specific advice on competency based interviews).

To do well you need to identify the important figures on the panel and what role they play, but never ignore anyone. Be prepared, it is more difficult to establish rapport with a group than with an individual. When you talk you should talk to the whole panel, make eye contact with everyone and, if your chair is in an awkward position, ask to move it slightly.

The chairperson will be the one making introductions but make plenty of eye contact with a person you'll be working with if you can identify them on the panel. Be prepared for rapid fire questions as candidates are often asked identical questions by panel members and they will have all their questions ready. This can result in the interview becoming a little 'clunky' and lacking flow, but don't be put off by this. Observe how people on the panel interact with each other to help you navigate through who is who in the decision making process.

HOT TIP

To do well you need to identify the important figures on the panel.

The behavioural or competency job interview

Behavioural, or competency job interviews, are increasingly common and, in my humble opinion, this is the area where genuine 'interview technique' applies. Standard interviews are not so much about technique, but actually about preparation and communication.

In a behavioural interview the interviewer asks specific questions seeking information about a candidate's skills, character and preferences based on examples of past behaviour. During the behavioural job interview, questions are directed toward specific experiences.

Our favourite description of an individual competence is a 'description of measurable work habits and personal skills used to achieve a work objective.' Some companies describe competencies as 'underlying characteristics, behaviours or skills required to differentiate performance' but, put simply, competencies are the key characteristics of the most successful performers that help them to be… well, successful.

Some examples:

"Tell me about a time when you had to deal with a difficult person at work."

"What proactive steps have you taken to make your workplace more efficient and productive? Specifically describe a policy, project or system you created or initiated."

"Describe a high pressure situation you had to handle at work. Tell me what happened, who was involved and what you did in terms of problem solving."

"Some situations require us to express ideas or opinions in a very tactful and careful way. Tell me about a time when you were successful in this type of situation."

059

Most people can give an example to most behavioural questions that they are asked, but the trick is to give your 'best' example. This is where preparation comes in. At the end of this book we have included some typical behavioural interview questions collected in key themes. With a little bit of thought, and by looking at the job description and person specification, you should be able to identify the key themes or competencies that the interviewer will be trying to evidence. To make this easier, go through the job description line-by-line, and picture yourself doing the job. What will the person in the role be responsible for? What are the likely challenges?

Once you've done this you can set about spending some time thinking about your example. For each responsibility or challenge, think about what examples from your past you can point to as 'supporting evidence' that you'd excel at the job, and write them down.

The key here is to spend at least a couple of hours on this. Our experience tells us that your first example will never be your best, so take the time to come up with at least two or three examples for each 'theme' that you have predicted you will be asked about. This also helps if one of your examples applies to more than one theme, as it will help if you don't regurgitate the same example over and over again.

HOT TIP

Behavioural or competency interviews are where technique is as important as anything else.

How to answer a behavioural interview question

Firstly, don't respond to a behavioural interview question with an extended pause or by saying something like, "wow, that's a good question." By all means, repeat the question out loud or ask for the question to be repeated to give you a little more time to think about an answer. Also, a short pause before responding is okay.

Use all your life experiences as examples for your answers.

When answering behavioural interview questions there are no right or wrong answers, so be honest. If you don't have an example for a question you're asked, don't try to make something up.

The S.T.A.R method

Though this structure will be familiar to some of you, I'll provide a quick recap here for the benefit of those who are unfamiliar. It's important that you understand this structure as it will allow you to provide a detailed, articulate answer for even the most complex question. It will also assist you in ordering your thoughts, if and when you happen to be surprised by a question that you haven't prepared for in advance.

SITUATION
TASK
ACTIONS
RESULT

S.T.A.R. – a recap

Situation:	Describe in a sentence or two what the initial scenario was.
Task:	List as a set of verbal bullet points, the tasks you identified that needed to be achieved.
Actions:	Describe the actions you took to complete the tasks, in particular identifying any obstacles you overcame with a brief description of how.
Result:	Describe the end result. Don't worry about a less than perfect outcome in your example, as long as you can talk about what you learned from it and how you have used this experience since.

The structure itself is fairly self explanatory and provided you follow it step-by-step, it should allow you to deliver a clear answer for whatever question is presented to you.

Question ?

Describe a situation where you had a conflict with another individual, and how you dealt with it. What was the outcome?

Answer !

Situation or Task

During a previous role I worked on a four person team that was ……. I got along with everyone quite well, except for one colleague. We disagreed strongly on the method we should use to …… My other teammates and I agreed on a course of action but he totally disagreed. He didn't budge on his position and even took passive-aggressive steps to prevent us from completing the project.

Action that you took

As a member of the team I set up an informal meeting. I simply asked him to explain his reasons for wanting to do the experiment his way. I just listened and asked questions to clarify. Some of his assumptions were clearly erroneous, but I knew pointing them out right away would just make him get defensive. After hearing him out, I had a better idea of where he was coming from and realised that he might have some misunderstandings on some basic concepts. I didn't think he would take too kindly to me correcting him, so I suggested that maybe we should set up a meeting with some other team members to discuss our different ideas and to see if he had any feedback or advice.

Result of the action

So we met with the other team members. We both presented our different reasons for wanting to do the experiment in a certain way. As predicted, the team brought up the faulty assumptions our stubborn teammate had, and that his method wouldn't be the best to use. He was obviously deflated, but he accepted the feedback and agreed to start using our method.

A QUICK WORD ABOUT *Psychometric testing*

Put simply, psychometric tests are a scientific way of measuring performance. They are often seen as a much more objective way of assessing people and are frequently included as part of an interview process (most often ahead of final interview stage).

Personality profiling tools are commonly used during psychometric testing. These often include personality questionnaires and assessments of motivation and emotional intelligence. Your profile, as described by these assessments, can change over time and is effected by a number of factors including, rather obviously, your emotional state, your current role (and how much you enjoy it and are challenged by it), your current Line Manager (and your relationship with them) and a range of external non-work related factors.

As these tests are, by design, objective in nature, you should never try to cheat or manipulate your answers to what you think they are trying to evidence (most psychometric tests have an inbuilt ability to spot if you try and do this!). Instead, cast your mind to a recent day when you felt motivated, challenged and energised by your work, your colleagues and your team. This will help to paint a picture of your 'best' self.

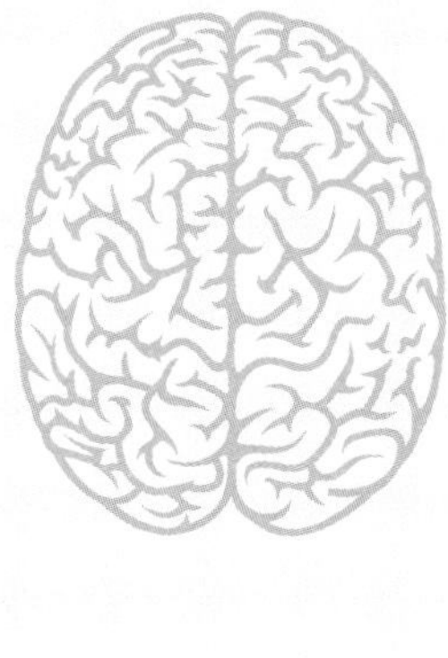

Other popular interview questions

THE **Top 10**

No two situations are ever exactly the same, but as a general guide, certain types of questions come up in a typical interview time and time again. Here is our guide to some of those specific questions and our advice as to the things that they are trying to evidence and how you should tackle them.

1 Tell me about yourself

The question (if not directly) will almost certainly come up. Not preparing a succinct, well thought out, high quality answer to this question is unforgiveable but very, very few executives do!

The subject that you know most about in the whole world is yourself and so most of us presume that, as we are subject matter experts on us, we don't need to think about this… but wait a minute. This is half about content and half about perception. Irrelevant, ramblings with no middle and no end to the story or the answer will give the interviewer a poor impression of you very early in the interview. You will be peddling up hill to recover for the next 50 minutes.

This question, often the interview opener, has a crucial objective: to see how you handle yourself in unstructured situations. The interviewer will want to see how articulate you are, how confident you are, and generally what type of impression you would make on the people with whom you come into contact on the job. The interviewer will usually also want to learn about the trajectory of your career (remember the importance of the narrative of a good story here, pointing to some desirable key aspects of your personal brand!).

065

1 Tell me about yourself (continued)

Your response should never take more than two to three minutes. When asked to tell them about yourself please do just tell them about yourself. DO NOT use this as an invitation to provide a monologue of everything they might want to know about why you are right for the job.

There are many ways to respond to this question correctly and just one wrong way: by asking, "What do you want to know?" The right response typically has three parts: focus on what interests the interviewer, highlight your most important accomplishments and prove that you are a human being.

Focus on what interests the interviewer

Do not dwell on your personal history - that is not why you are there. Start with your most recent employment and explain why you are well qualified for the position. The key to all successful interviews is to match your qualifications to what the interviewer is looking for. You want to be selling what the buyer is buying.

Highlight important accomplishments

Have a story ready that illustrates your best professional qualities. For example, if you tell an interviewer that people describe you as creative, provide a brief story that shows how you have been creative in achieving your goals.

Prove that you are a human being

This is the bit where you give a very brief overview of who you really are. Use your personal brand to give the briefest of pictures of what matters to you out of work. This should be easy but do give it some thought and a bit of craft to your answer.

Oh yes, and we do actually agree with you that attending Star Wars conventions dressed as Princess Leah at weekends is cool and that your collections of original 1950's bottle tops is one is the best in the North of England however, please understand that some people will find this just a bit weird, so it might not be the best place to start the interview. We are not joking, this does happen when people say "so tell me about yourself".

HOT TIP

A good interviewee will memorise a 60-second commercial that clearly demonstrates why he, or she, is the best person for the job.

2 How long have you been with your current (or former) employer?

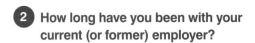

This is a 'hot-button' question if your CV reflects considerable job-hopping. The generally accepted view that excellent performers tend to stay in their jobs at least three to five years is being tested here.

If your résumé reflects jobs with companies that were acquired, moved, closed, or downsized, it is still viewed as a job-hopper's history.

Many of us have periods where our CVs have a few rapid fire career moves, so deal with the subject confidently and put the interviewer's mind at rest that you see their role as a long term opportunity.

3 What is your biggest weakness?

The key to responding to this question, perhaps rather obviously, is to avoid discussing characteristics critical to the position as a weakness. An impressive and confident response shows that the candidate has either prepared for the question or is seriously self-aware, has spent time on self-reflection, and can admit responsibility and accept constructive criticism.

Sincerely give an honest answer (but not a long one), be confident in the fact that this weakness does not make you any less of a great candidate, show that you are working on this weakness and tell the interviewer how. The best answers include how you have, or are, taking action to improve on your weaknesses and, in particular, what coping strategies you have employed to make sure that your employer or department isn't disadvantaged by this weakness.

4 Tell me about a situation where you did not get along with someone in your team

The wrong answer to this 'hot-button' question is, "I've been very fortunate and have never worked for or with someone I didn't get along with."

Everyone has had situations where they disagreed with a colleague or boss, and saying that you haven't forces the interviewer to question your integrity. Also, it can send out a signal that you are simply not seasoned enough or haven't been in situations that require you to develop a tough skin or deal with confrontation.

It's natural for people to have differing opinions. When this has occurred in the past, you could explain how you presented your reasons and openly listened to other opinions as well. The key to the best answers to this question lie in examples where you have used compromise, leadership and decision making to successfully navigate tricky work relationships. It is also a chance to display the ability and previous examples of placing organisational objectives ahead of your own.

5 Describe a situation where you were part of a failed project

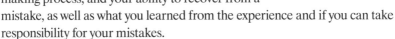

If you can't discuss a failure or mistake, the interviewer might conclude that you don't possess the depth of experience necessary to do the job. An interviewer is not looking for perfection, they are simply trying to better understand your level of responsibility, your decision-making process, and your ability to recover from a mistake, as well as what you learned from the experience and if you can take responsibility for your mistakes.

Respond that you'd like to think that you have learned something valuable from every mistake you have made. This ability to reflect and change your actions is powerful. Have a brief story ready with a specific illustration and even better have a follow up one that demonstrates what you learnt and how you didn't do the same thing the next time. It should conclude on a positive note, with a concrete statement about what you learned and how it benefited the company.

6 How do you explain your job success to date?

Be candid without sounding arrogant. Talented yet grounded is a good mode to be in here. Perhaps, mention observations other people have made about you, your work and your strengths and talents. If a previous failure has driven subsequent success, be bold and talk about it as this ability to reflect, learn, perceive and act is highly desirable. "I'm not sure, just right place, right time I suppose" is not a text book answer!

7 What do you do when you are not working?

The more senior the position, the more important it is that the interviewers know about the qualities that will impact on your leadership style. This links directly to the 'prove that you are a human being' part of the answer to question 1. The interviewer wants to try and judge whether you are well adjusted and happy, or a company zealot.

Discuss hobbies or pursuits that interest you, such as sports, clubs, cultural activities, and favourite things to read, all the time reinforcing your personal brand, and don't mention Princess Leah and 1950s Coke bottles!

8 What are your strengths?

The key to success is to demonstrate that you own strengths that are important to the specific job responsibilities. If the position requires scheduling or handling many deadlines, you should discuss your ability to multi-task, your use of collaboration or time management software, or give an example of a project you successfully managed.

Do not take this as an opportunity to open the flood gates and go through an exhaustive list of what makes the 'Super you'. Instead, describe two or three skills you have that are relevant to the job. Avoid clichés and generalities at all costs and make sure you offer specific evidence with examples answering the question of 'So what?' If you really want to do a bit of showboating, describe new ways these skills could be put to use in the position you are being considered for.

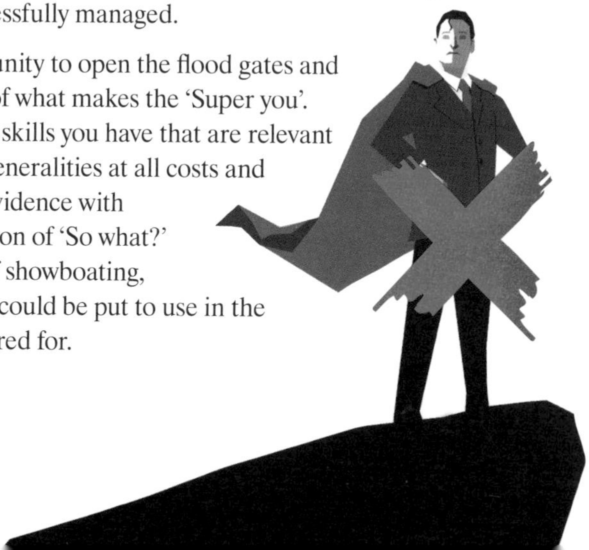

9 Why did you leave your last position?

Most leading executives have had a bad experience somewhere on their CV and it has probably contributed to their subsequent resilience and success.

Executive level roles demand that issues that relate to personality and temperament become more important than they might otherwise. The interviewer wants to know if you will fit in with their company and they may also be fishing for signs of conflict that indicate a potential personality problem.

It is important to keep your answer to this question positive. A negative response could indicate to the interviewer a lack of loyalty or consideration for the place you are leaving, immaturity or avoidance in owning your responsibility for issues and conflicts. An example of a positive response is, “The position allowed me to gain experience managing staff and working with senior executives. I am ready to expand my roles and level of responsibility and think this would be an interesting role”.

A QUICK WORD ABOUT
★ ★ ★
Dismissal
★ ★ ★

It is always awkward to let an interviewer know why you left your last executive job if you were laid off or especially if your employment was terminated. Be prepared to answer your layoff question with information that will dispel any assumption someone might have about cutting the poor performers. Try to show that there was a specific business reason behind your layoff. Your department was eliminated. The office was moved. The product you supported was being discontinued.

Be honest and straightforward, but do not dwell on any conflict that may have occurred. Highlight positive developments that resulted from your departure, whether it was that you accepted a more challenging position or learned an important lesson that helped you to be happier in your next job. DO NOT be tempted to lie about any embarrassing exit. Organisations change direction, are acquired and disposed of, and this typically leads to a change in executive resourcing. Deal with it and deal with it pragmatically and positively. Be warned, a lie at this stage will always be found out at some point.

10 Why do you want to work in this industry?

Provide proof that you aren't simply shopping in this interview. Make your passion for your work a theme that you allude to continually throughout the interview.

If you already work in the sector and you are changing employers, do exactly the same but demonstrate that you have made an assessment of their organisation and have a clear, well thought out rationale for being interested in their organisation. Accuracy of your view is the key here. A misguided or misinformed view about a sector or business will kill your chances of success, so take time to think about why you really want to be there.

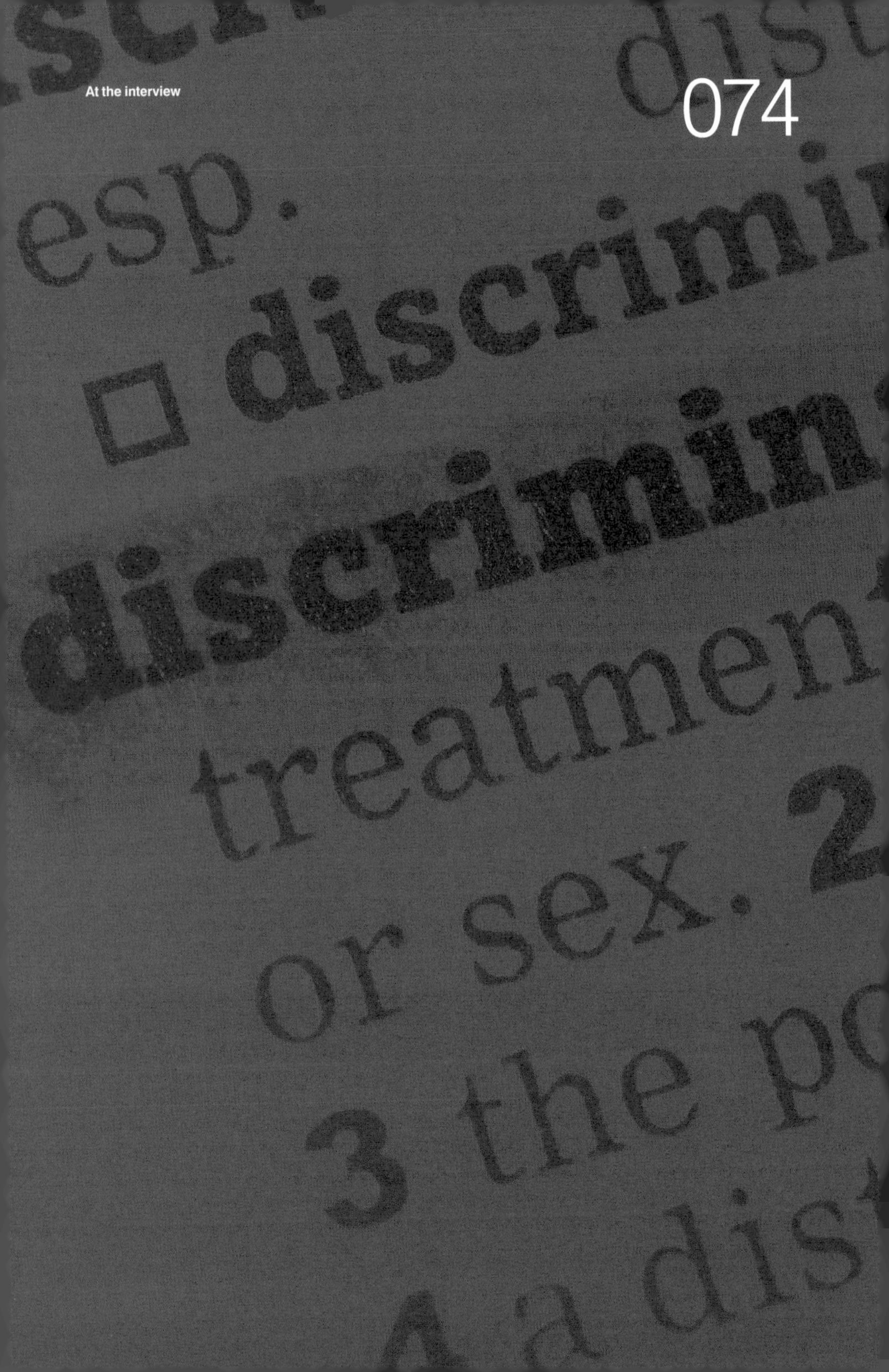
esp.
discrimin
discrimin
treatmen
or sex. 2
3 the po
a dist

A QUICK WORD ABOUT ★ ★ ★ *Discrimination* ★ ★ ★

Discrimination on the basis of race, marital status, colour, sex, religion, national origin or disability is not legal, no ifs or buts! Although thankfully very rare, it is possible that you may be faced with a question which is discriminatory, particularly from inexperienced interviewers. In these situations the best thing to do is to address the bias behind the question without confronting the interviewer, for example:

Are you planning to start a family?

- Are you asking if I am able to work overtime?
- Are you asking if I would have commitment to this position?

How old are you?

- Are you asking how many years of experience I have?

Needless to say, if you do encounter any discriminatory questions you have probably already decided that this wouldn't be the role or organisation for you, but knowing how to deal with them professionally and courteously, if they do ever appear, is a useful skill to possess.

076

The end of the interview

Usually the interviewer will signal when the interview is coming to an end. Try and use this as an opportunity to take the initiative.

Checking through your pre-prepared agenda you had wanted to share your experience in supply-chain management, however, the topic was never brought up. It is your responsibility to introduce it into the conversation. You might comment, "Before we end, I'd like to share one more thing with you that I think is important to the position and my fit within your organisation." Then proceed with the information. You must take the initiative during an interview to be sure you have communicated all that is of value.

077

When the interview has finally ended, establish what will happen next and who should do what. Be sincere in your thanks, even if you've been given a rough ride. Reinforce your interest in the job, even if you have some reservations. The objective is to be offered the position as you can always turn a job down once is offered!

"I'm very excited about this opportunity. What's our next step?"

This might very well be the deciding factor in getting an offer. And make sure that you actually SAY it in words at the end of the interview. Don't assume that they should have noticed your enthusiasm and interest level in this executive position from the rest of your comments during the interviewing process.

Establish what the next stage of the process is likely to be and what sort of timescales the interviewer is working towards. Now is also a good time to mention the subject of feedback. Something like:

"Thank you, I have really enjoyed this interview and have learnt a lot more about the position and organisation. I am obviously really keen however, should I not be successful, I would really value some feedback. If that is the case, what is the best way to do this?"

No, this isn't defeatist. The interviewer will probably have already made their mind up as to whether you will be coming back for another interview, so use this as an opportunity to try and line up some qualitative feedback. But, if you're asking for feedback, be prepared to deal with it. Egos are funny things and as well as not liking rejection, we tend to take details of that rejection pretty badly. Be pragmatic about this. Sometimes you did everything right and were just pipped to the post by someone working for a direct competitor that was just too good to turn down. Whether this is the case or not, anything you can glean as interview feedback will only serve to fine tune you for next time.

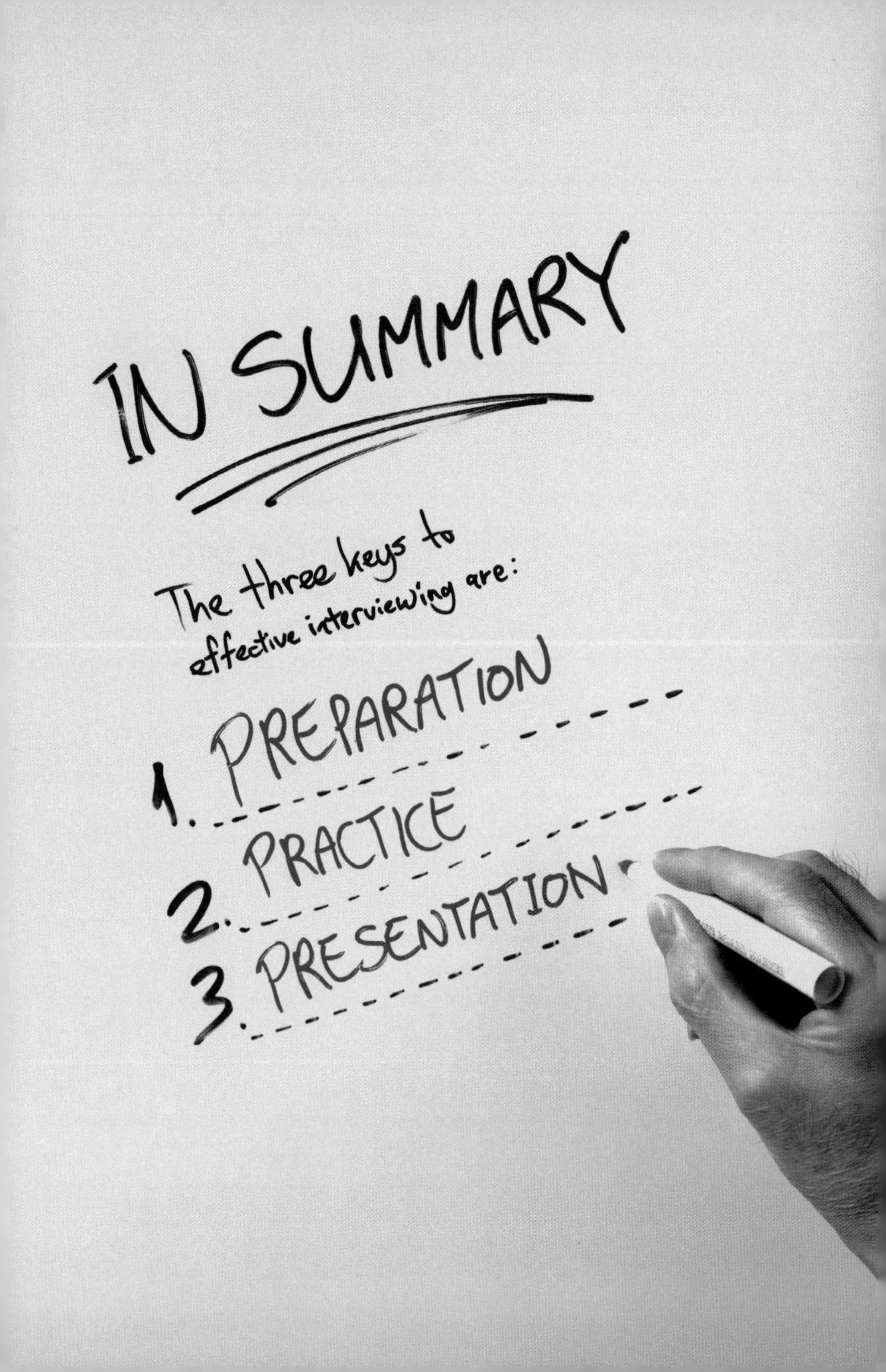
IN SUMMARY
The three keys to effective interviewing are:
1. PREPARATION
2. PRACTICE
3. PRESENTATION

1 Preparation

Prepare in advance of every interview

You simply cannot over-prepare for an interview. Those who prepare and take the time to do all their homework, put themselves at a major competitive advantage. Consider all the following steps in preparation for an up-coming interview:

Know the format

Confirm ahead of time the format of the interview. Will it be a phone interview, face-to-face interview, group interview, panel interview, lunch interview, dinner interview, etc? You NEVER want to be surprised by the format - it can definitely throw you off and affect your level of confidence.

Know the 'players'

Find out as much as you can about all of those individuals with whom you will be interviewing. Ask for their names in advance. If you're working with an Executive Recruiter, ask him or her to provide you with that information. Do a Google search on all of the individuals. Do a LinkedIn search on all of the individuals. Look for things in common with your background – former employers, college and university alumni, professional organisations, outside interests, etc. Draw up a list of possible talking points.

Know the position

Make sure you thoroughly understand the roles and responsibilities of the position for which you will be interviewed. Ask for a job description, find out why the position is open, thoroughly research similar positions on the internet (job boards are a great resource for this exercise). Confirm your understanding of the position with your key contact at the company. Make no presumptions about the position.

1 Preparation (continued)

Research the company

Thoroughly research the company. Talk to those in your network that know the company. Research the company on the internet. If a public company, review publicly available financial statement information. What are the key issues currently facing the company? Why is the position you are interviewing for available? Is it a new position? If so, why? Is it a replacement position? If so, what happened to the former executive employee? What are the company's key strengths? What is their market share for key products/services? What is going on with the company's key competitors? What late-breaking news is available on the company? Set up a Google Alert for the weeks/days leading up to your interview to keep current on late-breaking news.

Draw up insightful questions

Make a list of GREAT questions that you can ask. Formulate separate sets of questions for each of the individuals you'll be interviewing. Orient your questioning to each person's background, role and responsibility at the company. Remember... Great questions = Great candidates.

Draw up a list of questions that will likely be asked of you

Put together a comprehensive list of some of the key questions that you will likely be asked. What are the most difficult questions that you could be asked? Consider things such as: Gaps in your work experience; Short-tenure job positions (particularly those where you were employed less than one year; Lack of experience in one or more of the key requirements of the job position for which you will be interviewing.

2 Practice

This is the big one that most executive level candidates fail to give sufficient attention to. My experience in working with hundreds and hundreds of executives and preparing them for job interviews is that those who prepare almost always outshine their competition. Ideas for practice include:

- Role playing with a friend, your spouse, or an experienced coach.
- Self-observation. Practising in front of a mirror.
- Video replay. Video-taping yourself and critiquing your performance.
- Audio replay. Recording yourself and critiquing your performance.

As with anything, practice makes perfect. Why leave anything to chance? If the position you're planning to interview for is important, take the time to practise.

As an easy way into a practice session, why don't you get a friend, spouse/ partner, or someone you know well, to randomly ask some of the interview questions at the back of this book?

3 Presentation

Interview attire

Know the dress-style expectation ahead of time and take it up just a notch. If it's business casual and they ask you to dress business casual, then respect their request but take it up just a notch. For males that means putting a blue blazer over your golf shirt and wearing impeccable shoes.

Impeccable grooming speaks for itself.

Watch your manners

Show respect for everyone you meet; the Receptionist, the Administrative Assistant...everyone! It may be that everyone's vote counts. Be kind, be considerate, be nice.

Smile and be engaging

Interviews are serious, but let your personality come through. Smile and show enthusiasm. Be engaging. Practise an interview style that replaces 'stiffness' with being more conversational. Be interesting.

Avoid humour

Leave the joke-telling to others.

Appendix

Example Competency Based Interview questions

As an aid to your preparation we have attempted to cover some pretty typical competence areas and for each a number of example questions for you to practise. For the purpose of this appendix we have called these '**Level 1 competencies**' as they are very common.

We have also then covered some more idiosyncratic competencies which won't come up at every interview situation, but may well be areas that are tested for executive / leadership interviews. Again, for the purposes of this appendix we have called these '**Level 2 competencies**' purely because they are less common but are well worth familiarising yourself with. Remember, have a look at the competence area, have a think about a suitable example (your first example will usually not be your best) and then have a go at answering some of the questions using the S.T.A.R. method.

Good Luck!

Level 1 : Competencies

Interview competency – Communication

Communicates effectively, listens sensitively, adapts communication to audience and fosters effective communication with others.

Verbal

- Tell us about a situation where your communication skills made a difference to a situation.
- Describe a time when you had to win someone over, who was reluctant or unresponsive.
- Describe a situation where you had to explain something complex to a colleague or a client. Which problems did you encounter and how did you deal with them?
- What is the worst communication situation that you have experienced?
- How do you prepare for an important meeting?
- Tell us about a situation when you failed to communicate appropriately.
- Demonstrate how you vary your communication approach according to the audience that you are addressing.
- Describe a situation when you had to communicate a message to someone, knowing that you were right and that they were wrong and reluctant to accept your point of view.

Level 1 : Competencies

Listening

- Give us an example where your listening skills proved crucial to an outcome.
- Tell us about a time when you were asked to summarise complex points.
- Tell us about a time when you had trouble remaining focused on your audience. How did you handle this?
- What place does empathy play in your work? Give an example where you needed to show empathy?
- Describe a situation where you had to deal with an angry customer.

Written

- What type of writing have you done? Give examples? What makes you think that you are good at it?
- How do you feel writing a report differs from preparing an oral presentation?
- What positive and negative feedback have you received about your writing skills? Give an example where one of your reports was criticised.
- How do you plan the writing of a report?

Level 1 : Competencies

Interview competency – Conflict management

Encourages creative tension and differences of opinions. Anticipates and takes steps to prevent counter-productive confrontations. Manages and resolves conflicts and disagreements in a constructive manner.

- Tell us about a time when you felt that conflict or differences were a positive driving force in your organisation. How did you handle the conflict to optimise its benefit?
- Tell us about a time when you had to deal with a conflict within your team.
- Tell us about a situation where conflict led to a negative outcome. How did you handle the situation and what did you learn from it?
- Give us an example where you were unable to deal with a difficult member of your team.

Interview competency – Decisiveness

Makes well-informed, effective, and timely decisions, even when data is limited or solutions produce unpleasant consequences; perceives the impact and implications of decisions.

- What big decision did you make recently. How did you go about it?
- How did you reach the decision that you wanted to change job?
- Give an example of a time when you had to delay a decision to reflect on the situation. Why did you need to do this?

Level 1 : Competencies

- What is the decision that you have put off the longest? Why?
- When was the last time that you refused to make a decision?
- Give us an example of a situation where you had to make a decision without the input of key players, but knowing that these key players would judge you on that decision (e.g. superior unavailable at the time).
- Tell us about a time when you had to make a decision without knowledge of the full facts.
- Tell us about a situation where you made a decision that involuntarily impacted negatively on others. How did you make that decision and how did you handle its consequences?
- Tell us about a decision that you made, which you knew would be unpopular with a group of people. How did you handle the decision-making process and how did you manage expectations?
- Tell us about a situation where you made a decision too quickly and got it wrong. What made you take that decision?

Level 1 : Competencies

Interview competency – Delegation

Able to make full and best use of subordinate, providing appropriate support.

- What type of responsibilities do you delegate? Give examples of projects where you made best use of delegation.
- Give an example of a project or task that you felt compelled to complete on your own. What stopped you from delegating?
- Give an example of a situation where you reluctantly delegated to a colleague. How did you feel about it?
- Give an example where you delegated a task to the wrong person. How did you make that decision at the time, what happened and what did you learn from it?
- How do you cope with having to go away from the office for long periods of time (e.g. holidays)? Explain how you would delegate responsibilities based on your current situation.

Level 1 : Competencies

Interview competency – Influencing

Ability to convince others to own expressed point of view, gain agreement and acceptance of plans, activities or products.

- Describe a situation where you were able to influence others on an important issue. What approaches or strategies did you use?
- Describe a situation where you needed to influence different stakeholders who had different agendas. What approaches or strategies did you use?
- Tell us about an idea that you managed to sell to your superior, which represented a challenge.
- What is your worst selling experience?
- Describe the project or idea that you were most satisfied to sell to your management.
- Describe a time where you failed to sell an idea that you knew was the right one.

Level 1 : Competencies

Interview competency – Integrity

Ability to maintain job related, social, organisational and ethical norms.

- When have you had to lie to achieve your aims? Why did you do so? How do you feel you could have achieved the same aim in a different way?
- Tell me about a time when you showed integrity and professionalism.
- Tell us about a time when someone asked you something that you objected to. How did you handle the situation?
- Have you ever been asked to do something illegal, immoral or against your principles? What did you do?
- What would you do if your boss asked you to do something illegal?
- Tell me about a situation where you had to remind a colleague of the meaning of 'integrity'.

Level 1 : Competencies

Interview competency – Leadership

Acts as a role model. Anticipates and plans for change. Communicates a vision to a team.

- Tell us about a situation where you had to get a team to improve its performance. What were the problems and how did you address them?
- Describe a change where you had to drive a team through change. How did you achieve this?
- Describe a situation where you needed to inspire a team. What challenges did you meet and how did you achieve your objectives?
- Tell us about a situation where you faced reluctance from your team to accept the direction that you were setting.
- Describe a project or situation where you had to use different leadership styles to reach your goal.
- Tell me about a time when you were less successful as a leader than you would have wanted to be.

Level 1 : Competencies

Interview competency – Resilience and tenacity

Deals effectively with pressure; remains optimistic and persistent, even under adversity. Recovers quickly from setbacks. Stays with a problem/line of thinking until a solution is reached or is no longer reasonably attainable.

- Tell us about a situation where things deteriorated quickly. How did you react to recover from that situation?
- Tell us about a project where you achieved success despite the odds being stacked against you. How did you ensure that you pulled through?
- Tell us about your biggest failure. How did you recover and what have you learnt from that incident?
- Give us an example of a situation where you knew that a project or task would place you under great pressure. How did you plan your approach and remain motivated?
- How do you deal with stress?
- Give us an example of a situation where you worked under pressure.
- Under what conditions do you work best and worst?
- Which recent project or situation has caused you the most stress? How did you deal with it?
- Why did you last lose your temper?
- When is the last time that you were upset with yourself?
- What makes you frustrated or impatient at work?
- What is the biggest challenge that you have faced in your career? How did you overcome it?

Level 1 : Competencies

- Tell us about a time when you wanted to push one of your ideas successfully despite strong opposition.
- Which course or topics have you found most difficult? How did you address the challenge?

Interview competency – Teamwork

Contributes fully to the team effort and plays an integral part in the smooth running of a team without necessarily taking the lead.

- Describe a situation in which you were a member of team. What did you do to positively contribute to it?
- Tell us about a situation where you played an important role in a project as a member of the team (not as a leader).
- How did you ensure that every member of the team was allowed to participate?
- Give us an example where you worked in a dysfunctional team. Why was it dysfunctional and how did you attempt to change things?
- Give an example of a time when you had to deal with a conflict within your team? What did you do to help resolve the situation?
- How do you build relationships with other members of your team?
- How do you bring difficult colleagues on board? Give us an example where you had to do this.

Level 2 : Competencies

Interview competency – Compliance

Conforms to company policies and procedures.

- How do you ensure compliance with policies in your area of responsibility?
- Tell us about a time when you went against company policy. Why did you do it and how did you handle it?

Interview competency – Creativity / innovation

Develops new insights into situations; questions conventional approaches; encourages new ideas and innovations; designs and implements new or cutting edge programs/processes.

- Tell us about a project or situation where you felt that the conventional approach would not be suitable. How did you derive and manage a new approach? Which challenges did you face and how did you address them?
- Tell us about a situation where you trusted your team to derive a new approach to an old problem. How did you manage the process?
- Tell us about a time when you had to convince a senior colleague that change was necessary. What made you think that your new approach would be better suited?

Level 2 : Competencies

Interview competency – External / situational awareness

Understands and keeps up-to-date on local, national, and international policies and trends that affect the organisation and shape stakeholders' views; is aware of the organisation's impact on the external environment.

- Describe, through examples drawn from your experience, how you measure and take account of the impact of your decisions on external parties.
- Give an example where you underestimated the impact of your decisions on stakeholders external to your organisation.

Interview competency – Flexibility

Modifies his or her approach to achieve a goal. Is open to change and new information; rapidly adapts to new information, changing conditions, or unexpected obstacles.

- Describe a situation where you had to change your approach half-way through a project or task following new input into the project.
- Describe a situation where you started off thinking that your approach was the best, but needed to alter your course during the implementation.
- Describe a situation where one of your projects suffered a setback due to an unexpected change in circumstances.
- Describe a situation where you were asked to do something that you had never attempted previously.
- Give us an example of a situation where your initial approach failed and you had to change tack.

Level 2 : Competencies

- Describe your strongest and your weakest colleagues. How do you cope with such diversity of personalities?
- If we gave you a new project to manage, how would you decide how to approach it?

Interview competency – Independence

Acts based on his/her convictions and not systematically the accepted wisdom.

- When did you depart from the 'party line' to accomplish your goal?
- Which decisions do you feel able to make on your own and which do you require senior support to make?
- Describe a situation where you had a disagreement or an argument with a superior. How did you handle it?
- When do you feel that it is justified for you to go against accepted principles or policy?
- Which constraints are imposed on you in your current job and how do you deal with these?
- When did you make a decision that wasn't yours to make?
- Describe a project or situation where you took a project to completion despite important opposition.
- When have you gone beyond the limits of your authority in making a decision?

Level 2 : Competencies

Interview competency – Risk taking

Takes calculated risks, weighing up pros and cons appropriately.

- Tell us about risks that you have taken in your professional or personal life? How did you go about making your decision?
- What is the biggest risk that you have taken? How did you handle the process?
- Please describe one of your current or recently completed projects, setting out the risks involved. How did you make decisions? How do you know that you made the correct decisions?
- What risks do you see in moving to this new post?

Interview competency – Leveraging diversity

Fosters an inclusive workplace where diversity and individual differences are valued and leveraged to achieve the vision and mission of the organisation.

- Give an example of a situation or project where a positive outcome depended on the work of people from a wide range of backgrounds and ideas.
- Tell us about a time when you included someone in your team or a project because you felt they would bring something different to the team.

Level 2 : Competencies

Interview competency – Organisational awareness

Demonstrates an understanding of underlying organisational issues.

- Describe a project where you needed to involve input from other departments. How did you identify that need and how did you ensure buy-in from the appropriate leaders and Managers?
- Describe a time when you failed to engage at the right level in your organisation. Why did you do that and how did you handle the situation?

Interview competency – Sensitivity to others

Aware of other people and environment and own impact on these. Takes into account other people's feelings and needs.

- What problems has one of your staff or colleagues brought to you recently? How did you assist them?
- Tell us about an unpopular decision that you made recently? What thought process did you follow before making it? How did your colleagues/clients react and how did you deal with their reaction?
- How do you deal with 'time wasters'? Give a recent example.
- When is that last time that you had an argument with a colleague?
- When did you last upset someone?
- What steps do you take to understand your colleagues' personalities? Give an example where you found it hard to adjust to one particular colleague.